THERIZINOSAURUS

AND OTHER COLOSSAL-CLAWED PLANT-EATERS

Prehistoric World

THERIZINOSAURUS
AND OTHER COLOSSAL-CLAWED PLANT-EATERS

VIRGINIA SCHOMP

 **Marshall Cavendish**
Benchmark
New York

Contents

THE STRANGE "SCYTHE LIZARDS"

A small mousy mammal peeks through the ferns beside a pond in prehistoric Mongolia. It is the Age of Dinosaurs, and little animals must watch out for all the fierce hunters prowling the land. Yikes! Here comes a *Therizinosaurus*! One look at this giant's three-foot claws, and the tiny mammal dives for cover. But the dinosaur is not hunting for mouse meat. Instead, it has its eyes on the treetops. Stretching out its long arms, it pulls a tall branch toward its mouth. With a snap, its jaws chop off the leaves and twigs. Then the ferocious-looking dinosaur peacefully munches its salad-bar supper.

Many odd-looking creatures walked the earth during the Age of Dinosaurs. Strangest of all were the therizinosaurs, or "scythe lizards." These dinosaurs got their name from their huge bladelike claws. To fossil hunters, the claw of a therizinosaurus looked like a scythe, a kind of farm tool with a long curved blade.

Therizinosaurus *looked like a deadly predator, but most scientists think that this remarkable dinosaur mainly ate plants.*

A PUZZLING FAMILY

Paleontologists (scientists who study prehistoric life) had a hard time figuring out where the therizinosaurs fit into the dinosaur world. These puzzling animals had long necks and small leaf-shaped cheek teeth. That made them look like the prosauropods, a group of four-legged

Riojasaurus

Anchisaurus

plant-eating dinosaurs. But the "scythe lizards" walked on two legs. They had hollow bones, and they grasped objects with their hands. Those were features of the fierce meat-eating dinosaurs known as theropods.

In some ways, the puzzling therizinosaurs resembled prosauropods like this giant Riojasaurus *and its pint-sized cousin* Anchisaurus.

The paleontologists debated for a long time. Finally, most of them agreed that the therizinosaurs belonged to their own special group. The long-clawed dinosaurs were theropods that ate *plants* instead of *meat*. The chart on page 26 shows where the scientists placed these unusual theropods in the dinosaur family tree.

Most scientists believe that the therizinosaurs were closely related to two-legged meat-eating theropods like this fierce Utahraptor.

BIG AND BIZARRE

The largest and strangest member of the therizinosaur family was *Therizinosaurus.* This prehistoric monster looked like it was put together from a grab bag of mismatched parts. It had a big belly and a fairly short, fat tail. Its long neck ended in a small head with a toothless beak. It walked around on short stumpy legs and broad four-toed feet.

Most bizarre of all were the dinosaur's arms and claws. *Therizinosaurus* had huge arms packed with powerful muscles. Its hands were tipped with three curved claws measuring up to three feet. That's longer than a baseball bat. It's also longer than the claws of any other animal that ever lived.

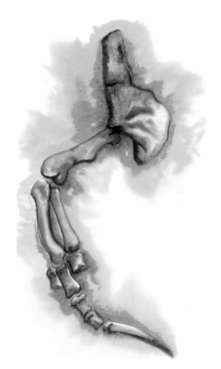

This fossil of a Therizinosaurus's arm is nearly eight feet long. At the bottom of the picture, you can see one of the dinosaur's huge curved claws.

THERIZINOSAURUS
(ther-uh-zeen-uh-SORE-us)
When: Late Cretaceous, 77–69 million years ago
Where: Central Asia
- About 20 feet long—half as long as a school bus
- Weighed about 3 tons—as much as a hippopotamus

Therizinosaurus *was a big, slow-moving, awkwardly built animal. One scientist said that it probably "looked like a half-plucked turkey and walked like a pot-bellied bear."*

A DESERT WORLD

*T*herizinosaurus lived mainly in the Gobi Desert of Mongolia, a region in central Asia. Seventy-five million years ago, the desert was a vast field of sand dunes dotted with lakes and streams. Trees, ferns, and other plants grew around the waters. The plants provided food for

The Age of Dinosaurs

Dinosaurs walked the earth during the Mesozoic era, also known as the Age of Dinosaurs. The Mesozoic era lasted from about 250 million to 65 million years ago. It is divided into three periods: Triassic, Jurassic, and Cretaceous. (Note: In the chart, MYA stands for "million years ago.")

────────── Mesozoic era ──────────

TRIASSIC PERIOD	JURASSIC PERIOD	CRETACEOUS PERIOD

250 MYA   205 MYA   135 MYA   65 MYA

230 MYA
First dinosaurs appear

Many types of
dinosaurs; first birds

77–69 MYA
Therizinosaurus

many different kinds of animals. There were lizards, frogs, birds, insects, and small furry mammals. But the most incredible creatures of this prehistoric land were the dinosaurs.

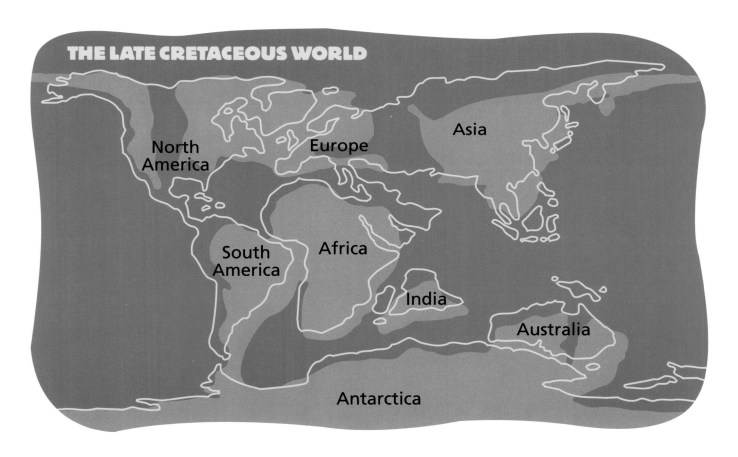

The face of the earth is always changing, as the continents slowly move. The yellow outlines on the map show the shape of the modern continents. The green shading shows their position about 75 million years ago, in the days of Therizinosaurus.

AMAZING NEIGHBORS

Let's take a tour of *Therizinosaurus*'s world. We must travel back to prehistoric Mongolia, toward the end of the Age of Dinosaurs. Our time machine lands among tall hills of sand. Beyond the dunes is a shallow green pond.

Some amazing animals have gathered by the water. We can see several colossal-clawed therizinosaurs reaching for the tall tree branches. A "bone-head" with a thick helmetlike skull is taking a drink. An ankylosaur covered with armor plates and spikes feeds on some low-growing plants. Speedy "ostrich dinosaurs" snap at the fish, while a small horned dinosaur rests in the sun.

A Bagaceratops *parent and baby warm themselves in the Mongolian sun.* Bagaceratops *was a horned dinosaur with one small horn on its nose. It was just three feet long and weighed about as much as a small dog.*

Mongolia is also home to many fierce meat-eating theropods. The scariest are the tyrannosaurs. Long powerful legs make *Alectrosaurus* one of the fastest of these deadly hunters.

Alectrosaurus *was a medium-sized tyrannosaur and an ancestor of Tyrannosaurus.* Although it was only half as big as its famous relative, it was still a very dangerous predator.

DINOSAUR DEBATES

How did *Therizinosaurus* live? What did it eat? Why did it have such humongous claws? Paleontologists have come up with many different answers to these questions, but no one knows for sure.

Some scientists think that the therizinosaurs used their long claws to rip open ant and termite mounds. The dinosaurs might have had sticky tongues, like today's ant-eaters, for lapping up the insects. Other experts disagree. They say that it would have taken an army of ants to fill up a three-ton *Therizinosaurus*!

> **SEGNOSAURUS**
> (seg-no-SORE-us)
> **When:** Late Cretaceous,
>   85–80 million years ago
> **Where:** Mongolia
> ◆ May have been as long as a
>   fire engine
> ◆ Name means "slow lizard"

Segnosaurus had short legs and short broad feet. Like all therizinosaurs, it was probably too slow to hunt other animals for food.

Some paleontologists have pictured the therizinosaurs as fish-eaters. They think that the dinosaurs swam or waded in the water and snagged their supper with their mouths and claws. The problem with this idea is that *Therizinosaurus* had a blunt toothless beak at the front of its snout. That would have been a clumsy tool for holding on to a slippery fish.

Most scientists have concluded that *Therizinosaurus* ate plants. The dinosaur could have used its claws like hooks to gather in branches. It probably snipped off the tender plant parts with its beak and ground them up with its small knobby cheek teeth.

The only complete skull of a therizinosaur that fossil hunters have found belonged to Erlikosaurus. *This dinosaur had rows of small leaf-shaped teeth and a toothless beak at the front of its upper jaw.*

ERLIKOSAURUS
(er-lick-oh-SORE-us)
When: Late Cretaceous,
85–78 million years ago
Where: Mongolia
◆ As long as a large car
◆ Weighed about as much
as a gorilla

HANDY BLADES

Therizinosaurus probably had another use for its oversized claws. This slow-moving dinosaur lived in a world filled with dangerous predators. When a hungry tyrannosaur threatened, the plant-eater's three-foot blades would have come in handy as defensive weapons.

Alxasaurus *and the other therizinosaurs may have used their fearsome-looking claws to fight off hungry meat-eating dinosaurs.*

ALXASAURUS
(ALK-suh-sore-us)
When: Early Cretaceous, 112–110 million years ago
Where: Mongolia
◆ Earliest known therizinosaur
◆ Many small teeth with rounded bumps

EGGS AND BABIES

Paleontologists have only found bits and pieces of *Therizinosaurus*. To get a more complete picture of this mysterious dinosaur, they must study its eggs. Several fossilized eggs containing the skeletons of unhatched baby therizinosaurs were found in China in the 1990s. The tiny bodies had big heads and long tails. There were miniature claws on the hands and feet. The teeth in the jaws were just a twenty-fifth of an inch long. By studying these remarkably well-preserved little skeletons, scientists were able to "fill in the blanks" and reconstruct a grown-up *Therizinosaurus*.

This is a model of a therizinosaur egg and baby. The artist based the model on the fossilized eggs and skeletons discovered in China.

UNSOLVED MYSTERIES

Many different kinds of dinosaurs appeared and died out during the long Age of Dinosaurs. The last *Therizinosaurus* died about 69 million years ago. Four million years later, all the remaining dinosaurs disappeared.

Today paleontologists work to unravel the mysteries of the prehistoric world. No creature from that lost world is more mysterious than *Therizinosaurus*. After years of study and debate, we still aren't completely sure what this bizarre dinosaur looked like or how it lived. Fossil hunters continue to search for clues beneath the sands of the Gobi Desert. Every new discovery adds one more piece to the puzzle of the colossal-clawed therizinosaurs.

> ### DEINOCHEIRUS
> (die-no-KIE-rus)
> **When:** Late Cretaceous,
> 75–65 million years ago
> **Where:** Mongolia
> - May have been as large as *Tyrannosaurus*
> - Name means "terrible hand"

Deinocheirus survived right up to the end of the Age of Dinosaurs. This therizinosaur's awesome arms measured eight feet from the shoulder to the tip of the claws.

Dinosaur Family Tree

ORDER

All dinosaurs are divided into two large groups, based on the shape and position of their hip bones. Most saurischians had forward-pointing hip bones, like lizards.

SUBORDER

Theropods were two-legged dinosaurs with hollow bones, grasping hands, and long curved claws. Most theropods were meat-eaters.

INFRAORDER

Tetanurans were theropods with stiffened (not flexible) tails.

FAMILY

A family includes one or more types of closely related dinosaurs. The therizinosaur family included plant-eating theropods with long arms and immense claws.

GENUS

Every dinosaur has a two-word name. The first word tells us what genus, or type, of dinosaur it is. The genus plus the second word are its species—the group of very similar animals it belongs to. (For example, *Therizinosaurus cheloniformis* is one species of *Therizinosaurus*.)

26

Scientists organize all living things into groups, according to features shared.
This chart shows one way of grouping the colossal-clawed plant-eaters described in this book.

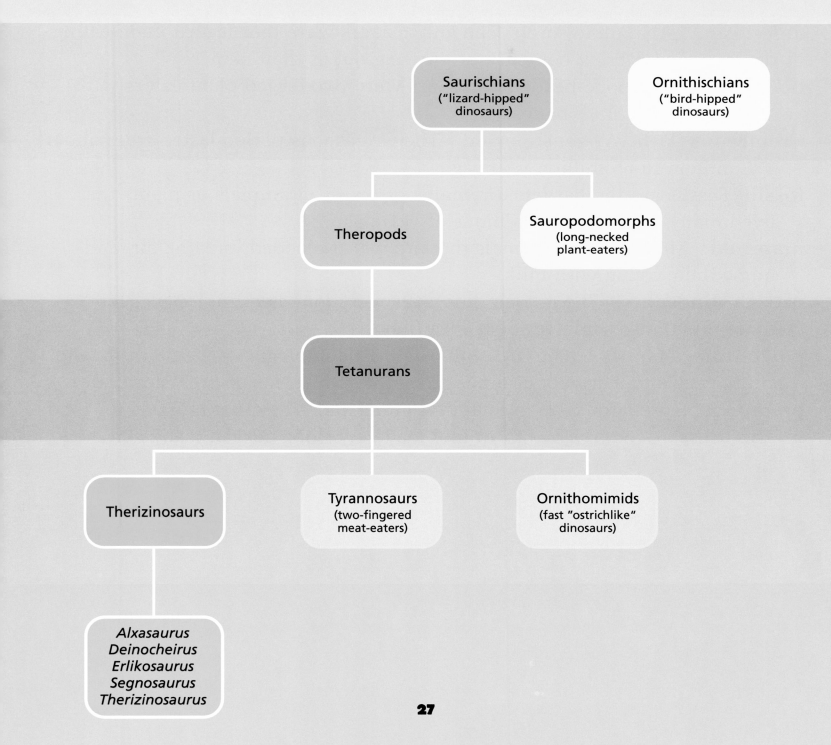

Saurischians
("lizard-hipped" dinosaurs)

Ornithischians
("bird-hipped" dinosaurs)

Theropods

Sauropodomorphs
(long-necked plant-eaters)

Tetanurans

Therizinosaurs

Tyrannosaurs
(two-fingered meat-eaters)

Ornithomimids
(fast "ostrichlike" dinosaurs)

Alxasaurus
Deinocheirus
Erlikosaurus
Segnosaurus
Therizinosaurus

Glossary

ankylosaur (AN-kuh-lo-sore): The ankylosaurs were four-legged plant-eating dinosaurs with thick bony armor growing out of their skin.

bone-head: The bone-headed dinosaurs were two-legged plant-eaters with large thickened skull bones.

Cretaceous (krih-TAY-shus) **period:** The Cretaceous period lasted from about 135 million to 65 million years ago.

fossil: Fossils are the hardened remains or traces of animals or plants that lived many thousands or millions of years ago.

mammal: Mammals are animals that are warm-blooded, breathe air, and nurse their young with milk.

ostrich dinosaurs: The ostrich dinosaurs were long-necked, long-legged dinosaurs that resembled today's ostriches.

paleontologists (pay-lee-on-TAH-luh-jists): Paleontologists are scientists who study fossils to learn about dinosaurs and other forms of prehistoric life.

predator: A predator is an animal that hunts and kills other animals for food.

scythe (sithe): A scythe is a farm tool made of a long curved blade attached to a long handle. It is used for cutting tall grains by hand.

therizinosaurs (ther-uh-ZEEN-uh-sores): The therizinosaurs were medium-sized to large plant-eating theropods with immense hand claws. They lived mainly in Asia during the Cretaceous period.

theropods: The theropods were two-legged dinosaurs with hollow bones, grasping hands, and long curved claws. Most theropods were meat-eaters.

tyrannosaurs (tie-RAN-uh-sores): The tyrannosaurs were large meat-eating dinosaurs with huge heads and long sharp teeth.

Find Out More

BOOKS

Barrett, Paul. *National Geographic Dinosaurs.* Washington, D.C.: National Geographic Society, 2001.

Lambert, David. *Dinosaur Encyclopedia: From Dinosaurs to the Dawn of Man.* New York: Dorling Kindersley, 2001.

Lessem, Don. *Scholastic Dinosaurs A to Z.* New York: Scholastic Books, 2003.

Marshall, Chris, ed. *Dinosaurs of the World.* 11 volumes. New York: Marshall Cavendish, 1999.

Rey, Luis V. *Extreme Dinosaurs.* San Francisco, CA: Chronicle Books, 2001.

Zimmerman, Howard. *Dinosaurs! The Biggest, Baddest, Strangest, Fastest.* New York: Atheneum Books for Young Readers, 2000.

ONLINE SOURCES *

Canadian Museum of Nature **at http://nature.ca/notebooks/english/mon2.htm**
This museum's online "Natural History Notebooks" provide interesting facts about nearly 250 types of animals. Click on "Prehistoric Life" for articles on *Therizinosaurus* and many other dinosaurs.

Dino Dictionary **at http://www.dinodictionary.com**
The "Dino Dictionary" profiles more than three hundred dinosaurs, including *Therizinosaurus* and several of its long-clawed relatives. You can click on the dinosaurs' names to hear how they are pronounced.

*Web site addresses sometimes change. The addresses here were all available when this book was sent to press. For more online sources, check with the media specialist at your local library.

Dino Directory at http://internt.nhm.ac.uk/jdsml/dino
The Natural History Museum in London, England, presents this guide to more than one hundred dinosaurs. Click on "Name A–Z" for information on therizinosaurs including *Deinocheirus, Segnosaurus,* and *Therizinosaurus.*

Dino Russ's Lair at http://www.isgs.uiuc.edu/dinos
Created by geologist Russ Jacobson, this Web site offers an excellent collection of links to museums and other organizations providing online information on dinosaur-related topics.

Jurassic Park Institute at http://www.jpinstitute.com/index.jsp
Created by Universal Studios, this entertaining Web site offers lots of information for dinosaur fans, along with great art and sound effects. Enter "Dinopedia" to print out "Flash Cards" for *Therizinosaurus* and hundreds of other dinosaurs.

Walking with Dinosaurs at
http://www.bbc.co.uk/dinosaurs/chronology/65/index_special.shtml
This companion site to the BBC television series *Walking with Dinosaurs* presents in-depth information on more than sixty dinosaurs through sound, video, photographs, and interactive games. Click on "Therizinosaurus" for a Fact File and video clip.

Index

About the Author

Virginia Schomp grew up in a quiet suburban town in northeastern New Jersey where eight-ton duck-billed dinosaurs once roamed. In first grade, she discovered that she loved reading and writing, and in sixth grade she was voted "class bookworm," because she always had her nose in a book. Today she is a freelance writer who has published more than fifty books for young readers on topics including animals, careers, American history, and ancient cultures. Ms. Schomp lives in the Catskill Mountain region of New York State with her husband, Richard, and their son, Chip.

Dinosaurs lived millions of years ago. Everything we know about them—how they looked, walked, ate, fought, mated, and raised their young—comes from educated guesses by the scientists who discover and study fossils. The information in this book is based on what most scientists believe right now. Tomorrow or next week or next year, new discoveries could lead to new ideas. So keep your eyes and ears open for news flashes from the prehistoric world!

Marshall Cavendish Benchmark
99 White Plains Road
Tarrytown, New York 10591-9001
www.marshallcavendish.us

Text copyright © 2006 by Marshall Cavendish Corporation
Map copyright © 2006 by Marshall Cavendish Corporation
Map and Dinosaur Family Tree by Robert Romagnoli

Library of Congress Cataloging-in-Publication Data
Schomp, Virginia.
Therizinosaurus : and other colossal-clawed plant-eaters / by Virginia Schomp.
p. cm. — (Prehistoric world)
Includes bibliographical references and index.
Summary: "Describes the physical characteristics and behavior of
Therizinosaurus and other colossal-clawed plant-eaters"—Provided by publisher.
ISBN 0-7614-2007-X
1. Therizinosaurus—Juvenile literature. 2. Dinosaurs—Juvenile literature. I. Title. II. Series.
QE862.S3S3867 2005
567.912—dc22
2004027719

Front cover: *Therizinosaurus*   Back cover: *Erlikosaurus*   Pages 2–3: *Alxasaurus*

Front and back cover illustrations courtesy of Marshall Cavendish Corporation
The illustrations and photographs on the following pages are used by permission and through the courtesy of Marshall Cavendish Corporation: 2–3, 6–7, 8–9, 10–11, 15, 16–17, 18, 19, 20–21, 22, 25; De Agostini/Natural History Museum Picture Library, London: 4–5; Jan Sovak: 12; Joe Tucciarone of Interstellar Illustrations: 13; Mark Thiessen / National Geographic Image Collection: 23

Printed in China

1 3 5 6 4 2